My College

My ESOL READERS

Set One: Book 2

My College
My ESOL Readers: Set One: Book 2
ISBN: 978-1-84231-381-7

Text by Rama Rangan
Edited by Bethan Bligh
Illustrations by Lucy Massey

Text copyright © 2025 Rama Rangan
Illustrations copyright © 2025 Gatehouse Books
All rights reserved

First published and distributed in 2025 by Gatehouse Books
Printed by Short Run Press, Exeter, Devon, UK

British Library Cataloguing-in-Publication Data:
A catalogue record for this book is available from the British Library

No part of this publication may be reproduced in any form or by any means, electronic, mechanical, photocopying, recording or otherwise, without the prior written consent of the publishers.

I am Abdul.

I live in Warrington.

I study at Warrington and Vale Royal College.

My college is very big.

There is a very big car park.

There are many classrooms.

There is a café.

There is a library.

There are many computers and laptops in college.

There are many teachers in our college. They are very good.

There are many other people who work in our college.

I learn English at college.
Our classroom is very big.

There are many tables, chairs and boards in our classroom.

I have many friends in college.
I really enjoy my time in college.

I like my college very much.

Author

Rama Rangan is an ESOL tutor at Warrington & Vale Royal College. She has been a teacher for more than 15 years. Rama speaks six languages and is learning two more! Rama was inspired to write these books as a learning aid for her students. She has used specific vocabulary and familiar references to make them relevant and engaging.

Editor

Bethan Bligh is Library Manager at Warrington & Vale Royal College. She champions the benefits of reading and promotes the correlation between reading and literacy.